*This book is dedicated to
the smiling faces we pass on
the street, the children whose
laughter warms our hearts,
and to the many good and
unselfish people of the world
who do their best to make a
difference.*

ISBN: 1467961418
ISBN-13: 978-1467961417

Thoughts on Life

Volume Two

Experience learning and learn from experience

When the ground drops from under you, it is time to fly

Bad things happen to those who look for them

When God sends you messages- be sure to pay attention

It's not the outfit, it's how you feel wearing it

Old and rusty may eventually be valuable

Trust takes time to build,
but can be destroyed in
seconds

If you cause others pain,
you will experience pain
yourself

Your real family are
those who love you no
matter what and show it

*Friendship is shown in
actions, not just words*

----

*Unconditional love has
no conditions*

----

*Your child's smile brings
hope for the future*

You take a chance by deciding too fast and miss a chance by deciding too slow.

Work outside to rest inside

An office should be the place for your work and have reminders of the reasons you are there.

*Beauty in nature is God's
business card*

----

*A parent's kiss or hug
should never be rejected*

----

*Children teach their
parents what their
parents forgot to teach
them*

Guilt is God's way of telling you when you are wrong

Invite someone to make the world better

What is the smell of fresh air?

*A good restaurant is best
when in good company*

----

*Without clouds and
seasons, each day would
be the same*

----

*To feel the wind in your
face, you must first
uncover your head*

Sometimes you learn
right from wrong by
making a mistake

If you don't have dreams,
they can't come true

Reach for the sky, but be
sure your pants stay up

You can say a lot in a few words

To know the good, you have to experience the bad

Text your words or say your thoughts

When you live in your
own world, you miss out
on the rest of the universe

If you follow the crowd,
you can't be sure where
you are going

Live life,
accept death

Whether it is too hot
or too cold
depends on what
you are used to

Don't assume you
understand.
Ask a question to be sure.

Balance allows you to
move ahead without
falling

Success is when you can provide for yourself and help others too.

Don't do work for work's sake

Remembering a fun time as a child will help you smile as an adult

Reward yourself when
you deserve it and
reward others when they
deserve it too.

You can make miracles
happen with a little help
from God

A man sent on an errand
will come back with what
he thinks she wanted
rather than what she
wanted

*Empty hands do not
mean an empty heart*

---

*You have to stand outside
before you can go inside*

---

*Don't say you can't when
you haven't tried or
know you can*

Enjoy the sun while it is shining

Your heart will stay empty until you decide to fill it

To appreciate the simple things in life, think like a dog

The best songs often bring
back the best memories

The most obvious things
are sometimes the most
difficult to see

Anywhere can be a
classroom if that is where
you learn

*Not knowing leads to
creation*

----

*You may wish you could
get back that which you
have thrown away*

----

*Time on your hands is
better than a weight on
your shoulders*

If the love is gone,
It wasn't there to begin
with

It takes time to turn a
mountain
into a sandy beach

A picture may be worth
a thousand words, but a
feeling can be more than
words can say

To know God is to
know the world

A tattoo on your body is
not as permanent as your
first love is on your heart

You don't always need a
reason to do something
with your life

*Think positive
to be positive*

----

*The best people have the
best friends*

----

*Don't say it can't get
much worse,
Instead say it's going to
get better.*

People need to be happy

----

*You aren't
communicating if
you make people guess*

----

*It's difficult to forgive
someone if they
don't regret what they
have done*

*True friends don't
separate
you from your real
friends*

---

*Do not overcomplicate
the simple things in life*

---

*Remember the path you
choose may not be the
best one for you, so choose
carefully*

God's whisper can do
more than all of
mankind's shouts

Sometimes it's easier to
just do it yourself

Witness compassion
Warm your heart

*A leader never gets lost
in the crowd*

---

*You don't need to teach a
child how to play, only
adults*

---

*When God's creatures
turn to you for help,
don't disappoint them.*

Natural disasters are natural occurrences

----

*Curiosity may have killed the cat,
but it put man on the moon*

Patience will eventually be rewarded... but are we patient enough to wait for it?

*Appreciate what God
shares with you*

----

*Make the world better
because
it is the only one we have*

----

*Use what you need and
share the rest*

*Fresh cut grass brings
good memories
and bad allergies*

All stress is self inflicted

----

*God's creatures are born
innocent.
What we do to them takes
it away.*

A gift made by hand is a gift from the heart

The tree with the most fruit has to work hardest to stand tall

----

Your boss may be stupid, but be thankful he hired you

*The first item in a
woman's grocery cart is
usually her purse*

----

*How does one describe
happiness?*

----

*What is so practical
about a practical joke?*

Youth has cries of laughter while maturity has tears of joy

It is better to watch out for trouble than to look for it

Fast food gives you time to eat more.

Will it matter in ten years?

When work is bad, just do your job and take the paycheck

Treat adults like children and they will become children

The wind can destroy but can also set you free

Make your children proud and they will make you proud

The things you cannot buy are the most precious

Ever-changing clouds
reflect ever-changing life

Listen to the silence to
hear your heart

You will never really
know when
you've reached your
destination

*Instead of sharing
frustrations,
try sharing new
experiences*

---

*Lending a hand is always
better than throwing a
stone*

---

*Don't ask someone else to
do something for you that
you should do for
yourself.*

*Don't test your faith-
trust in it.*

----

*Preventing something
bad may enable
something good*

----

*Problems cannot be
solved by neglect or
arguments*

*Just because you think
something is done, it
doesn't mean it is
finished.*